Dachshunds

Coloring book

Hand-drawn illustrations specially designed for this book.

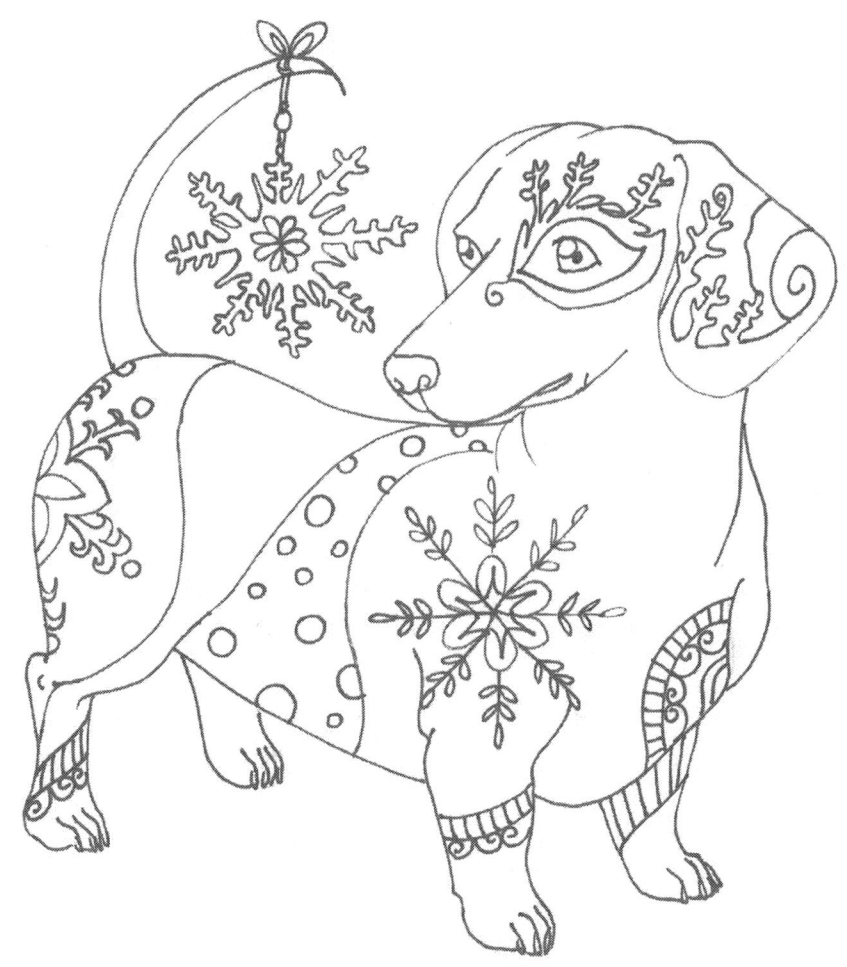

Christmas Edition

Illustrated by Micaela Rocío Mezzadra

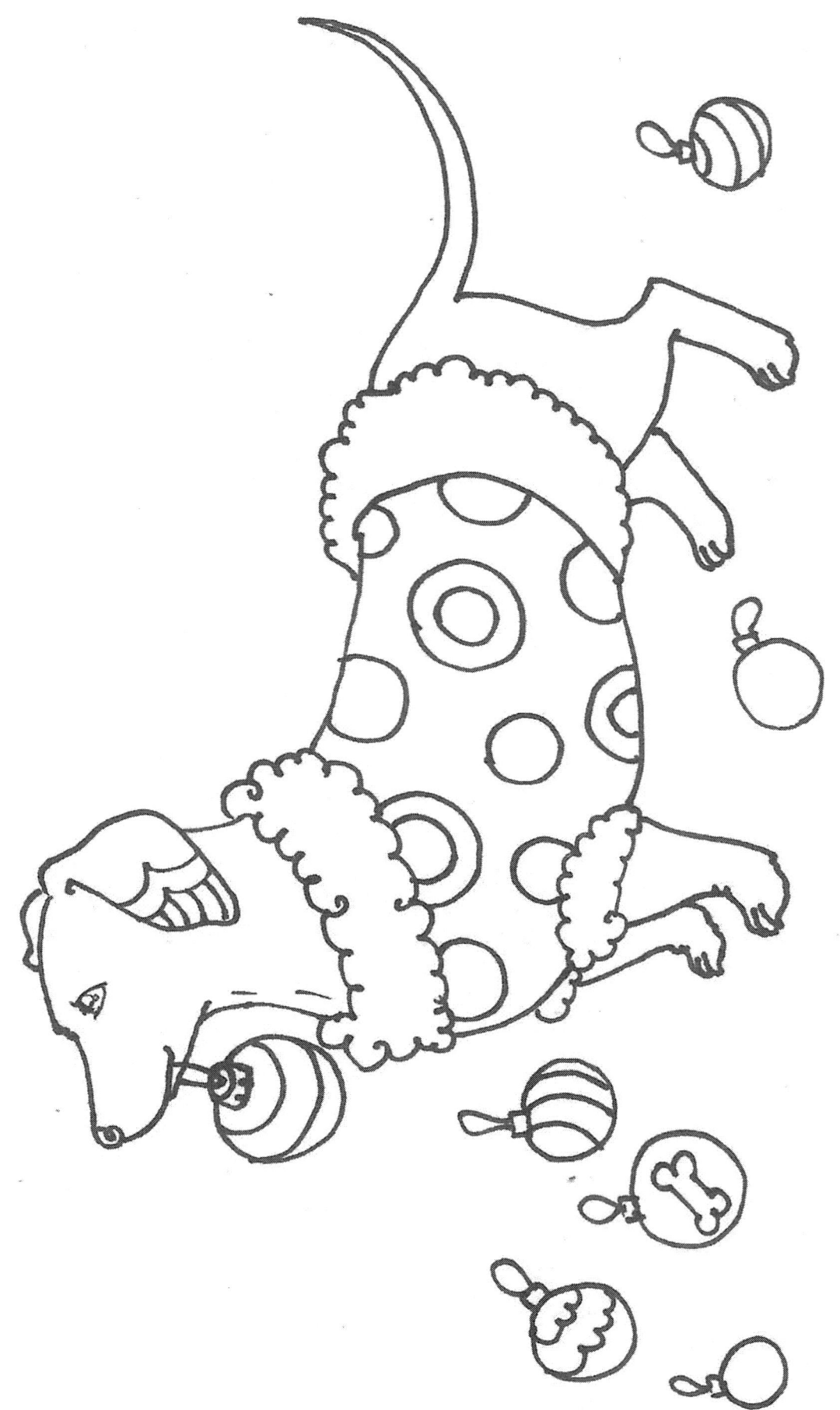

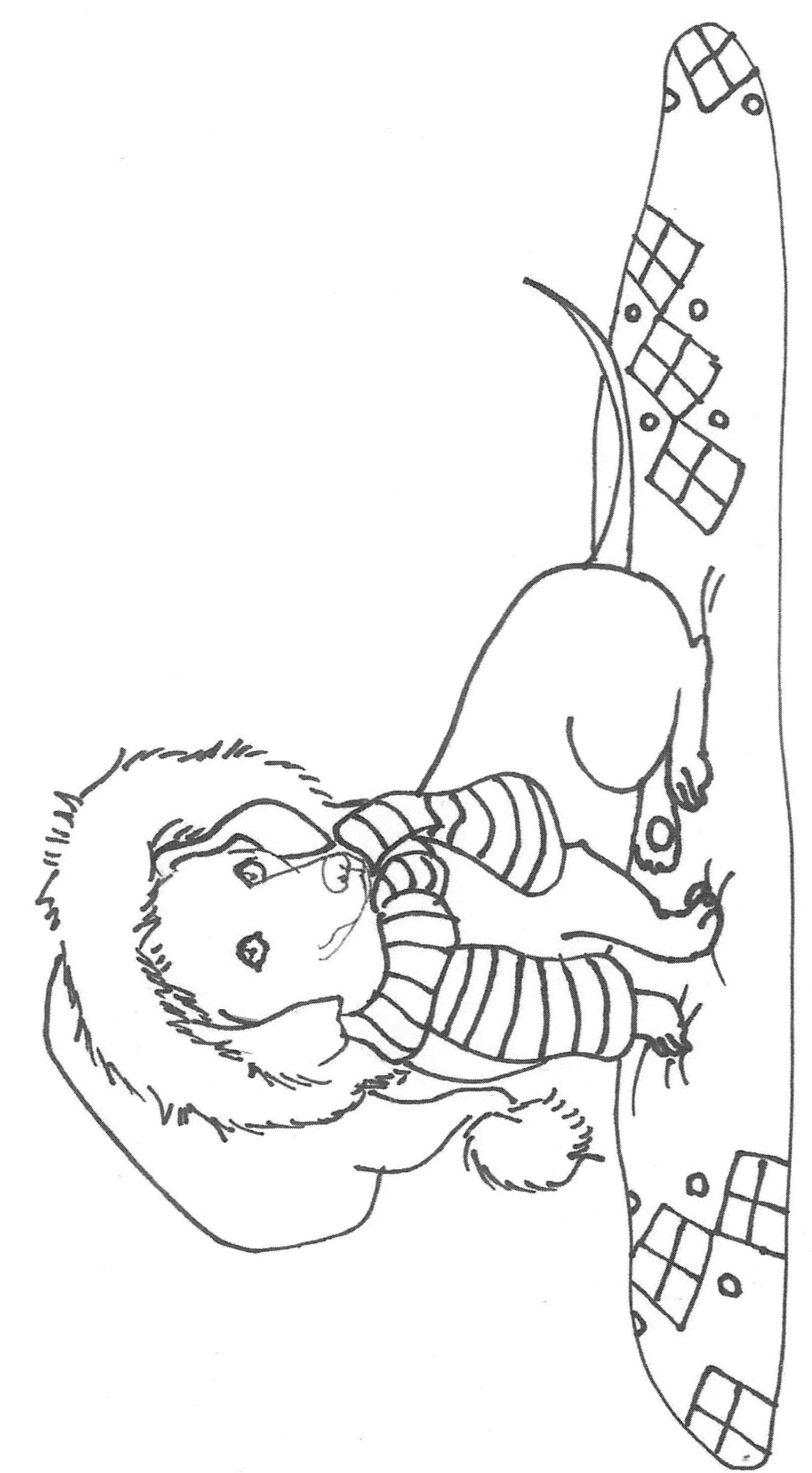

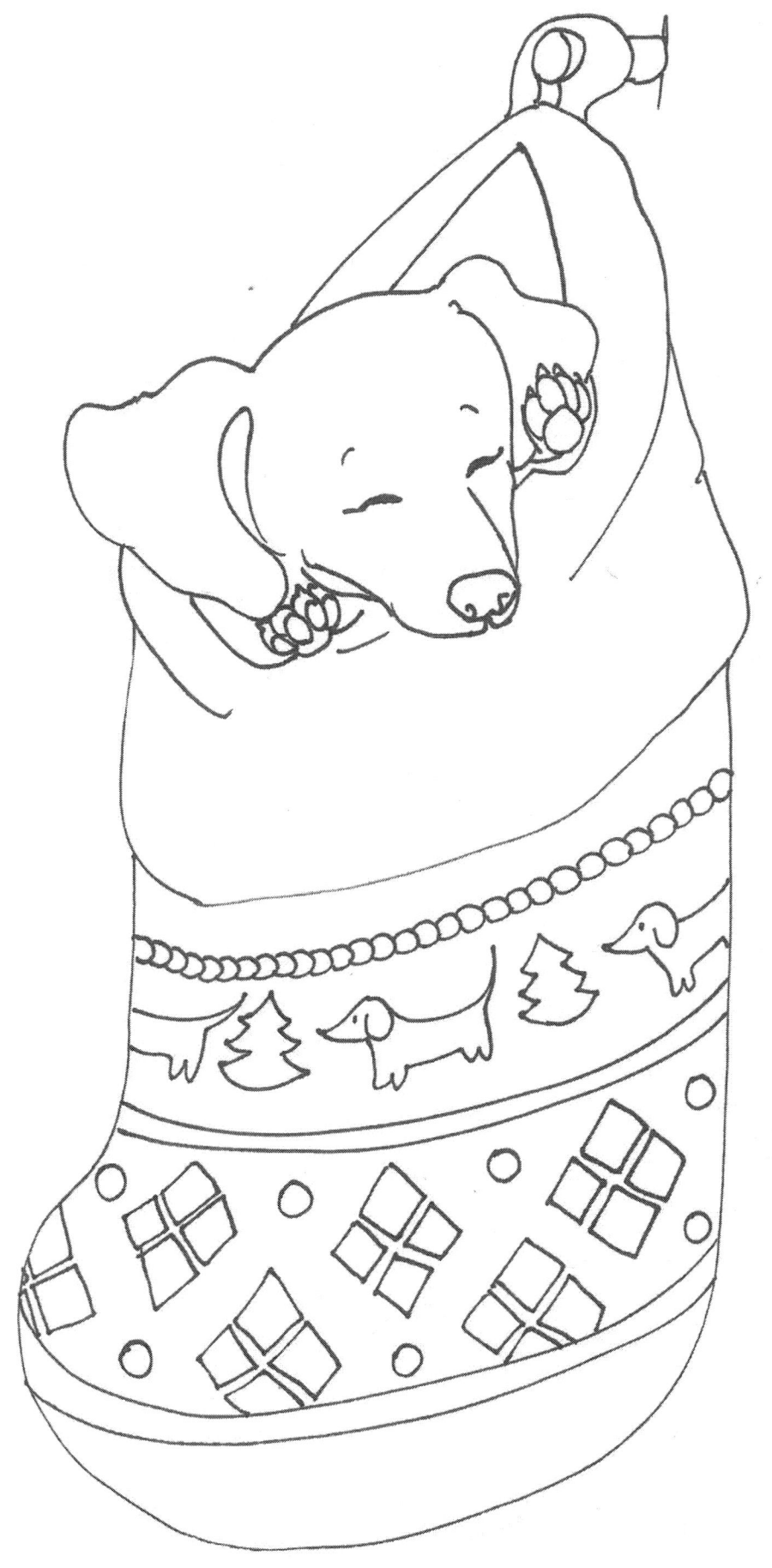

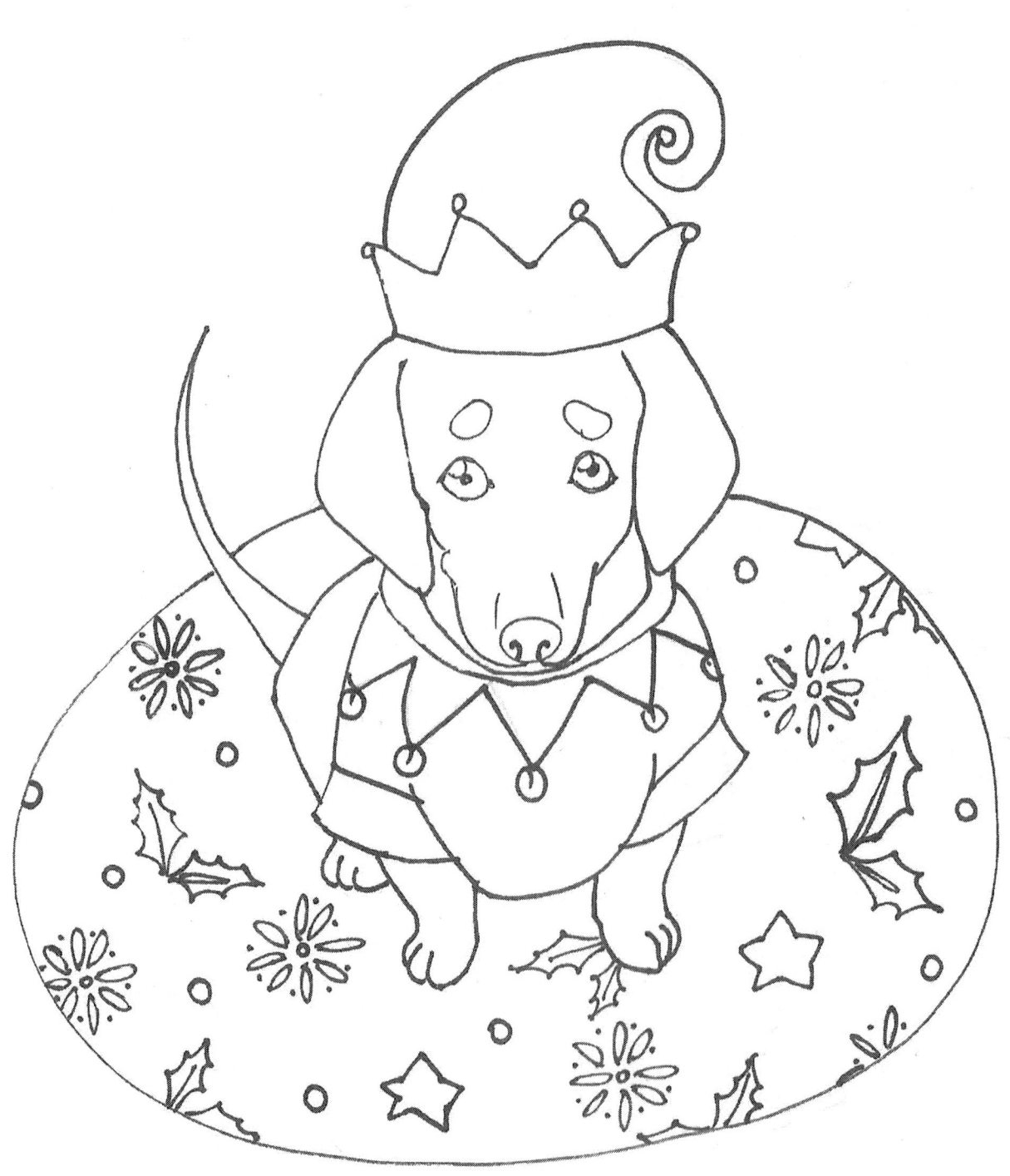

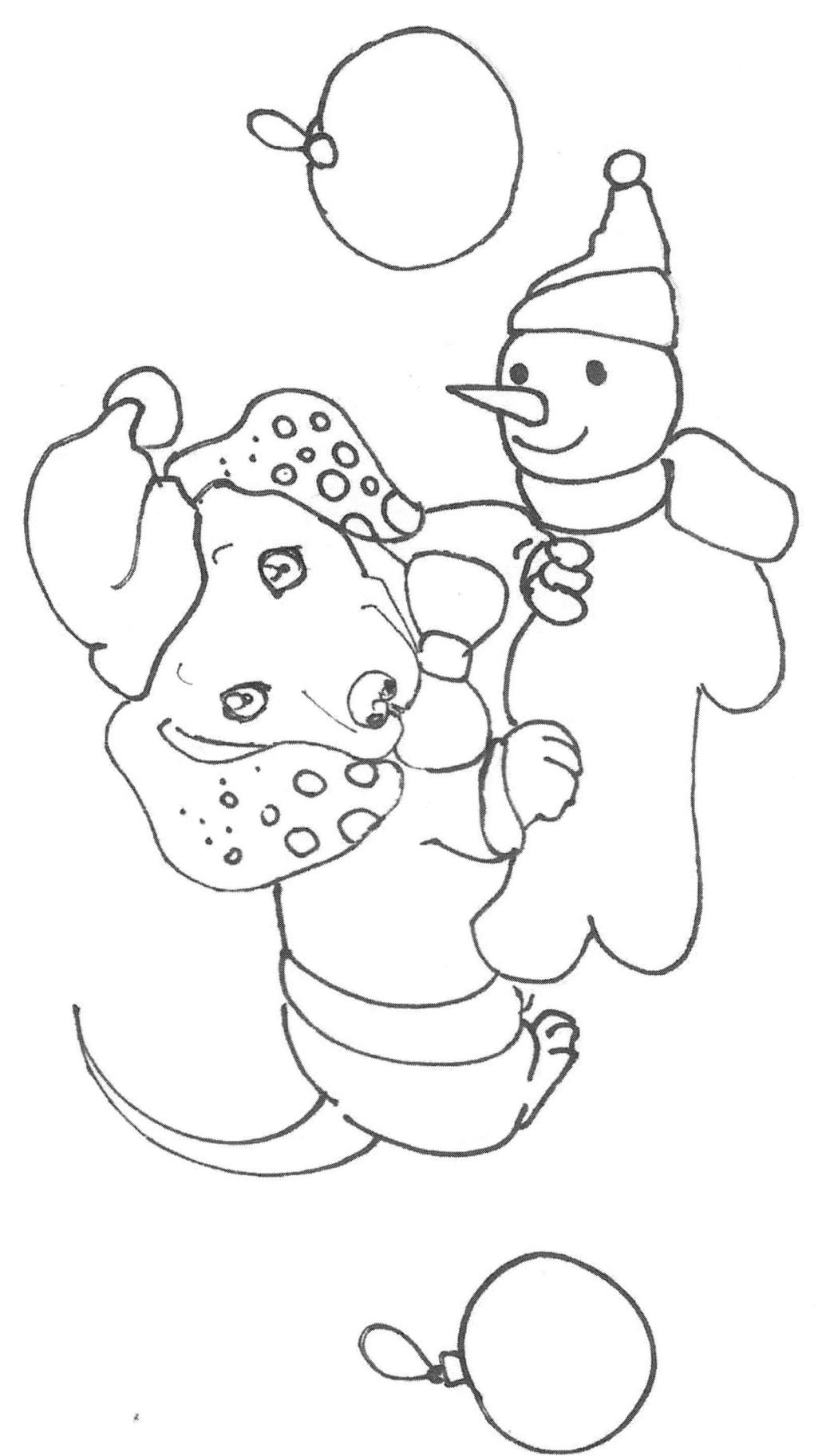

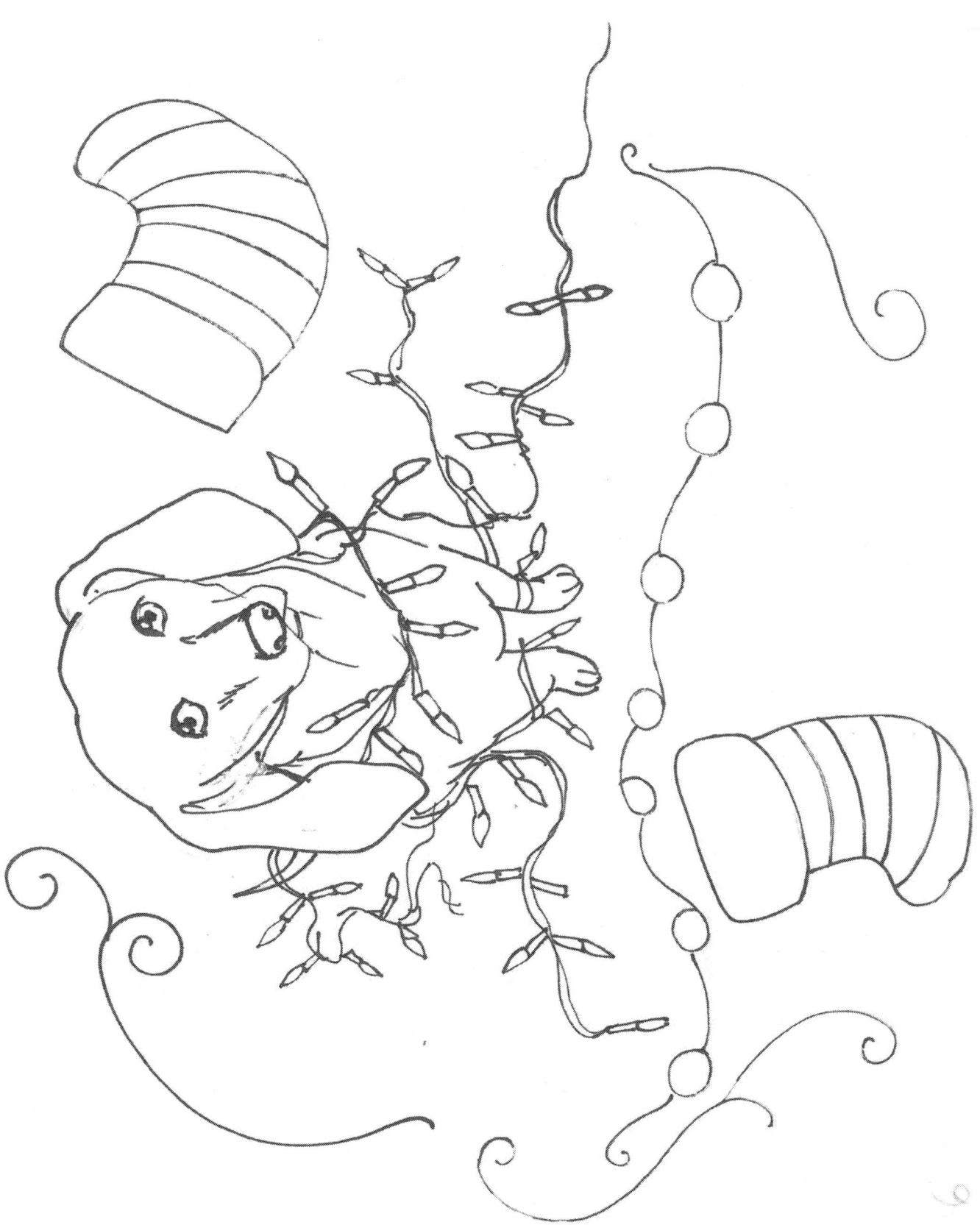

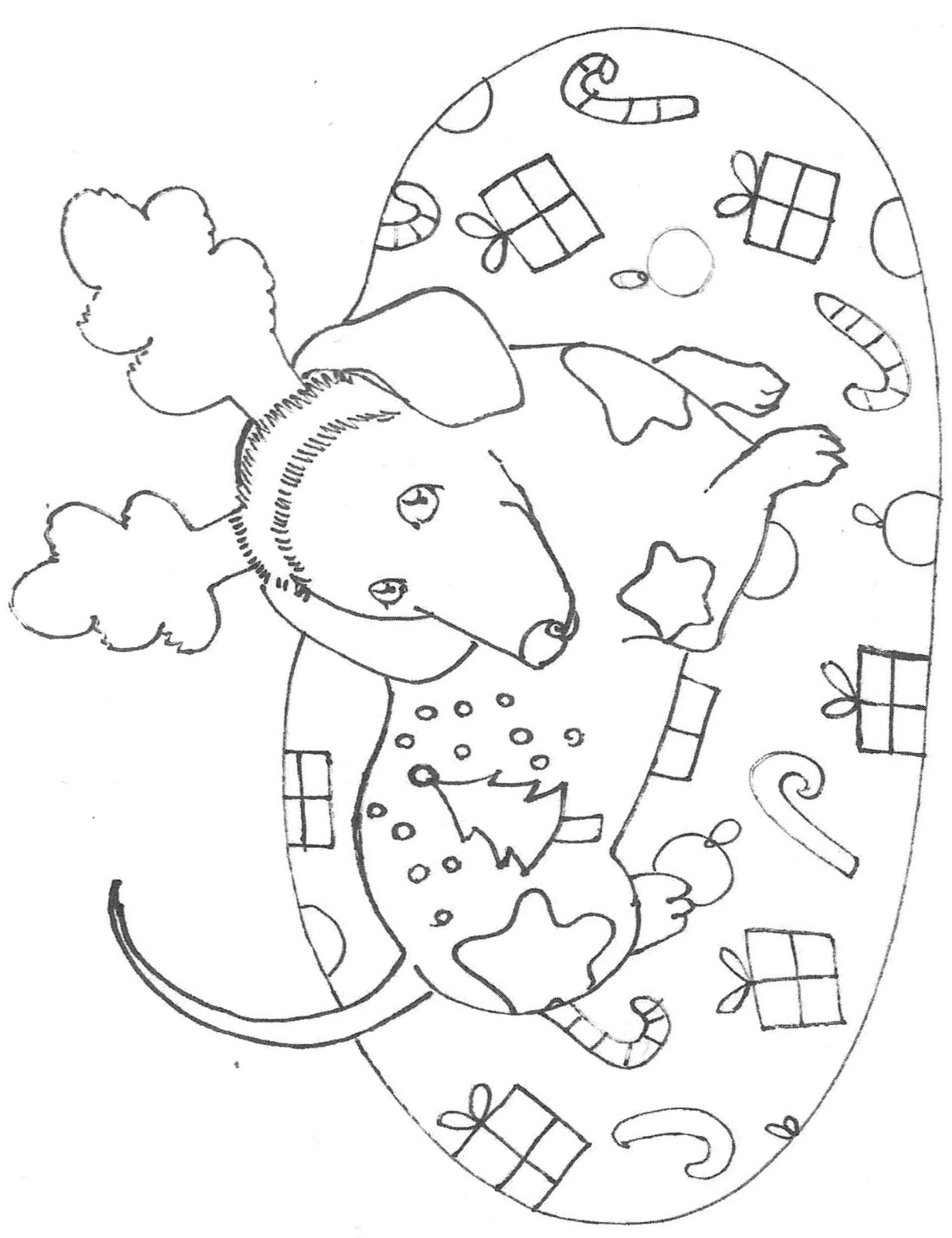

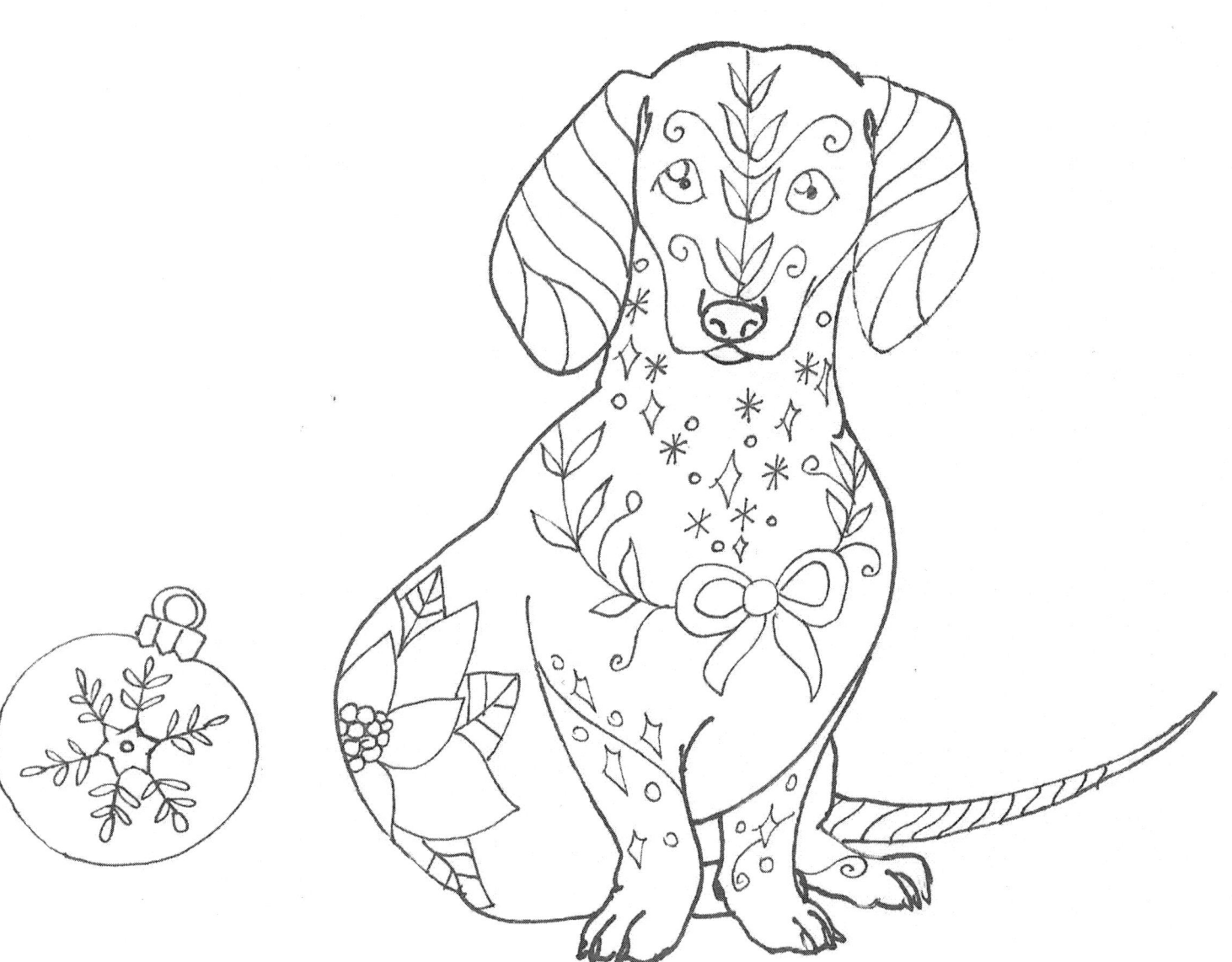

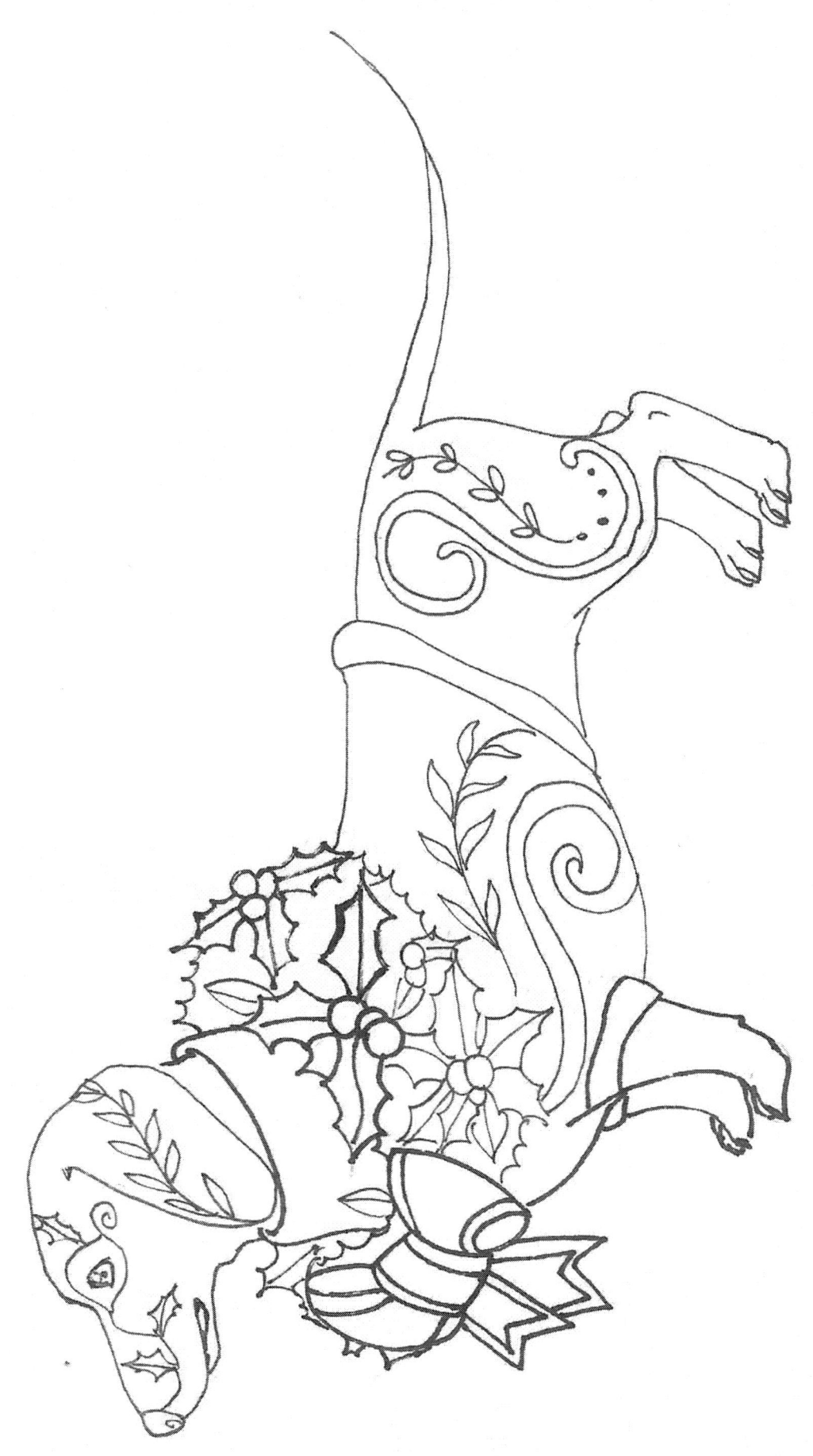

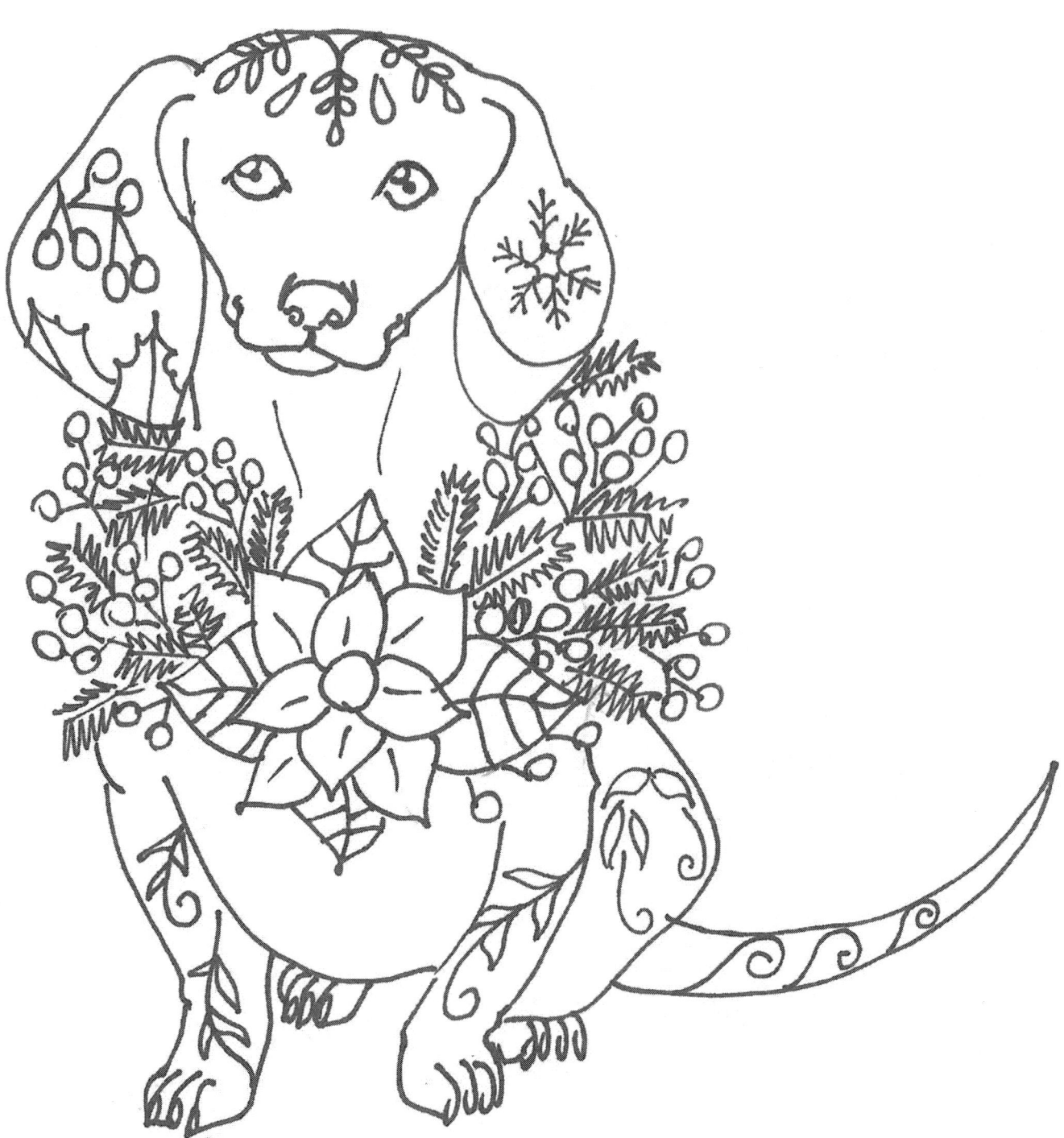

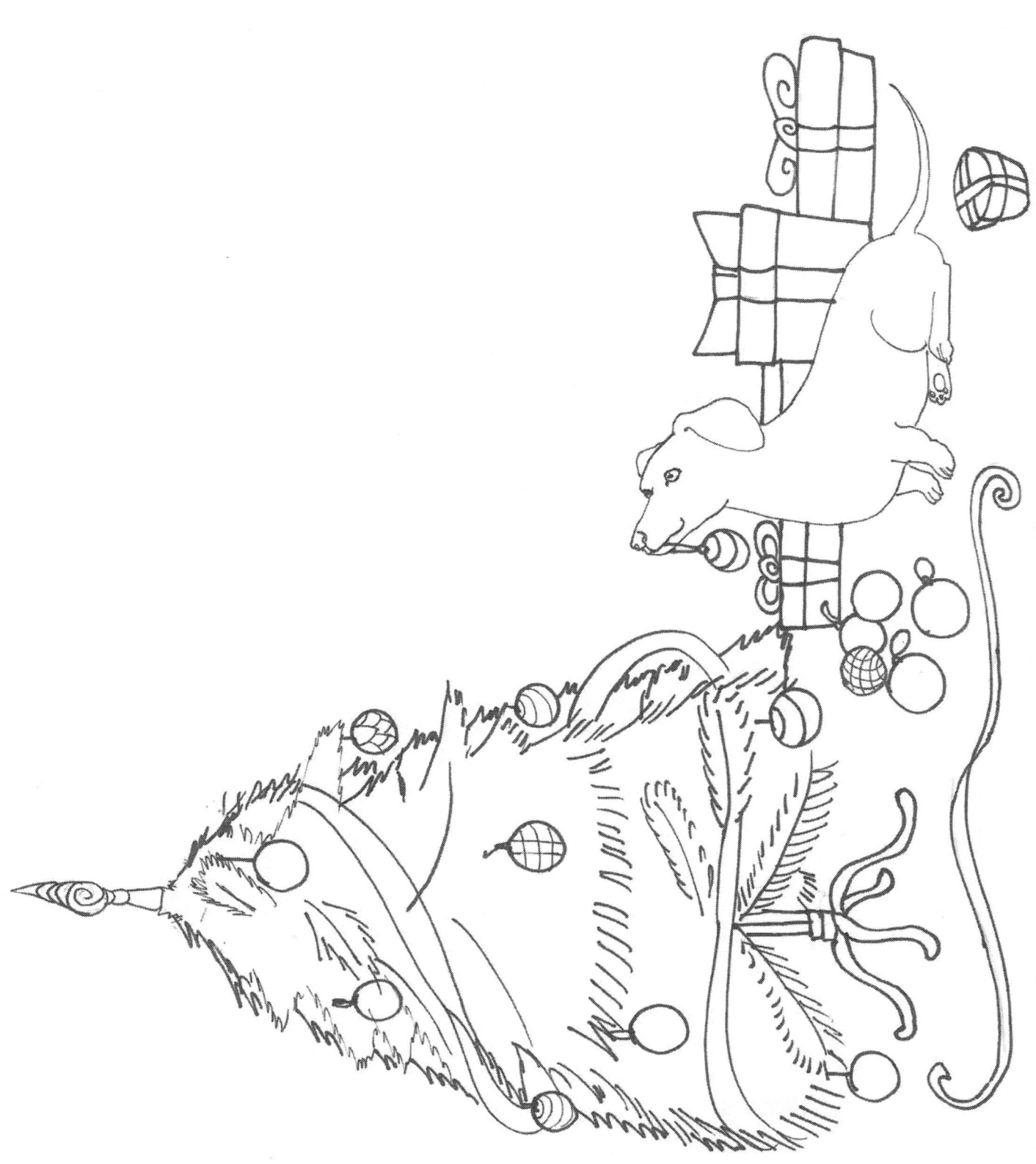

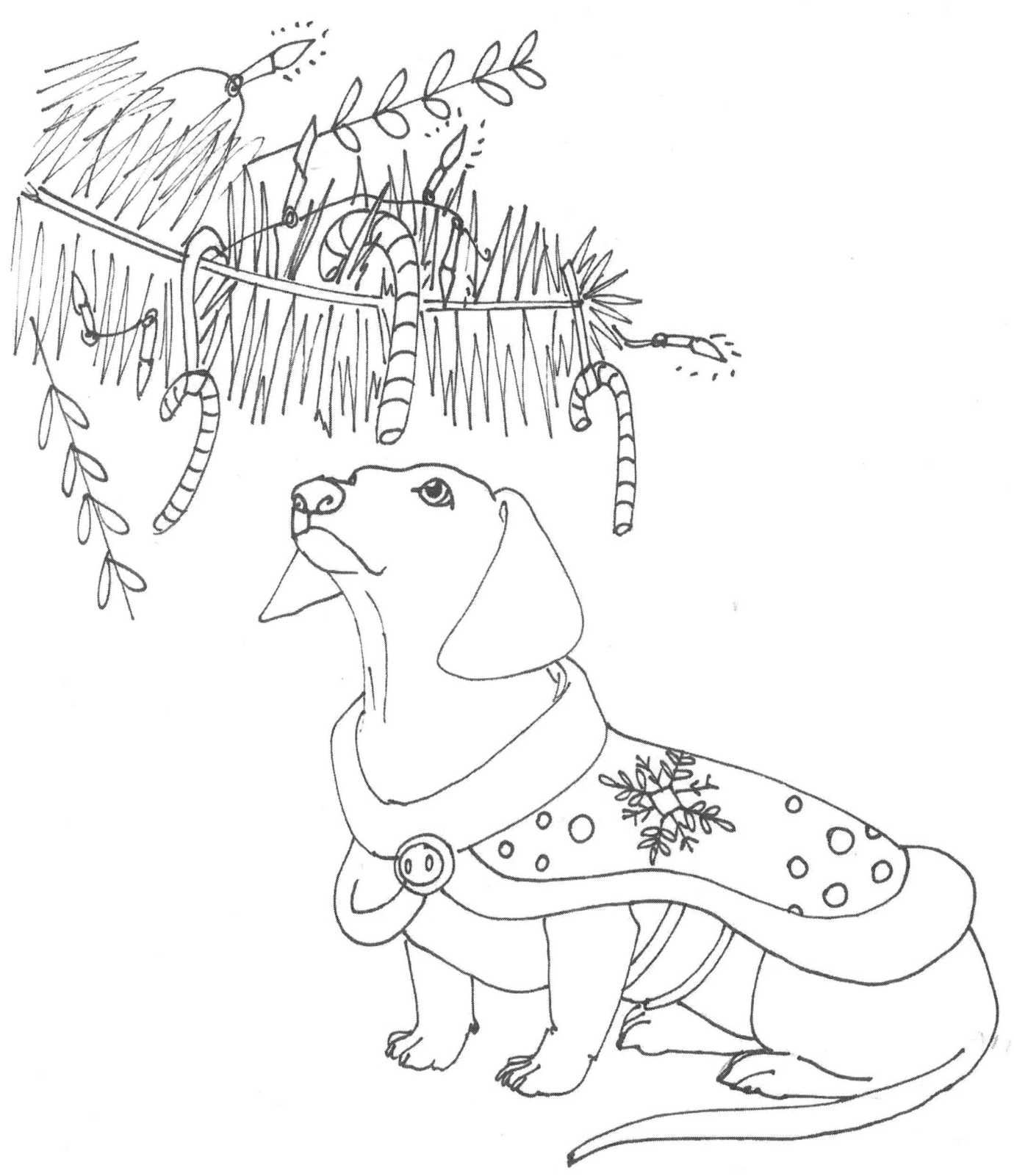

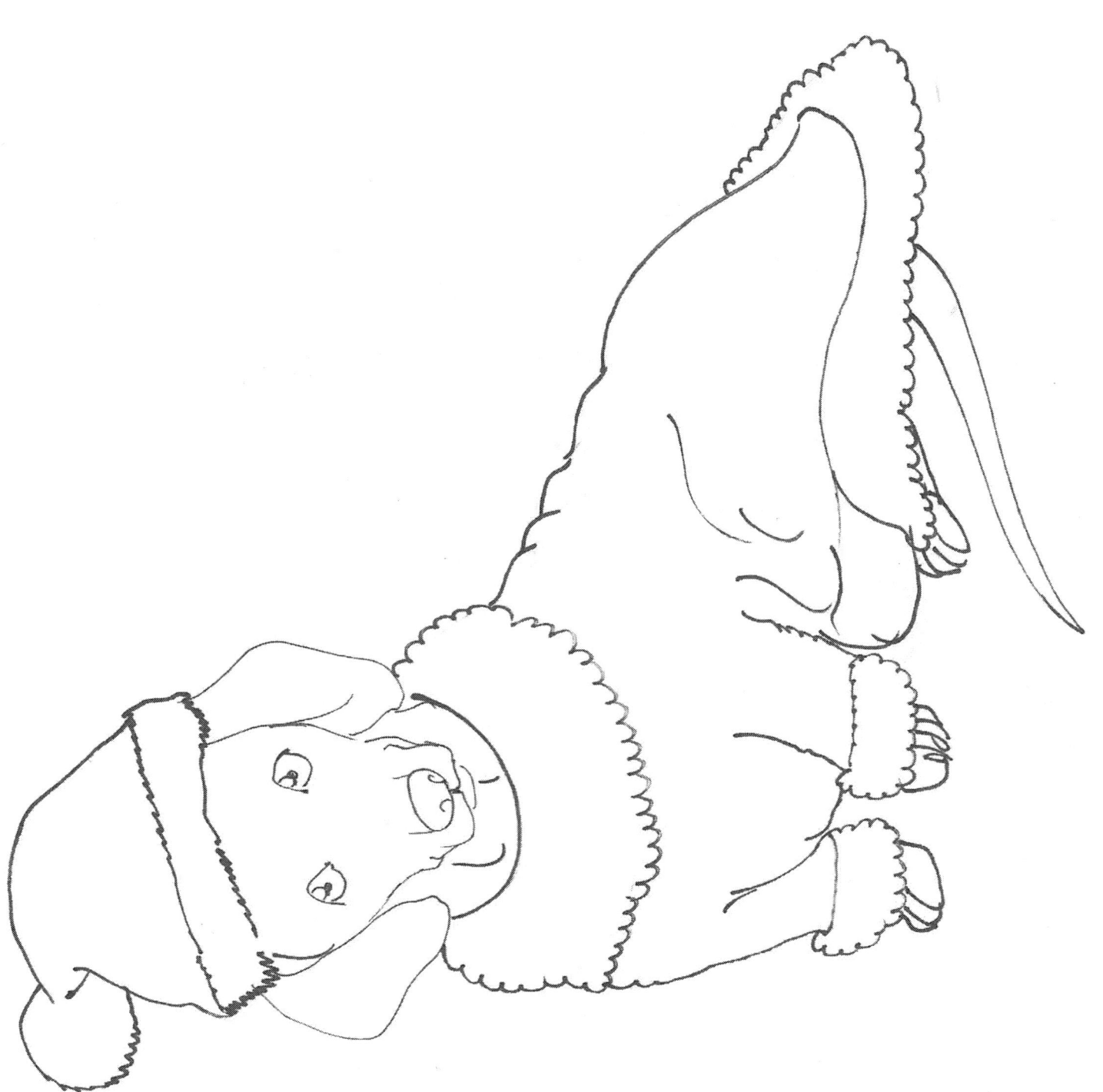

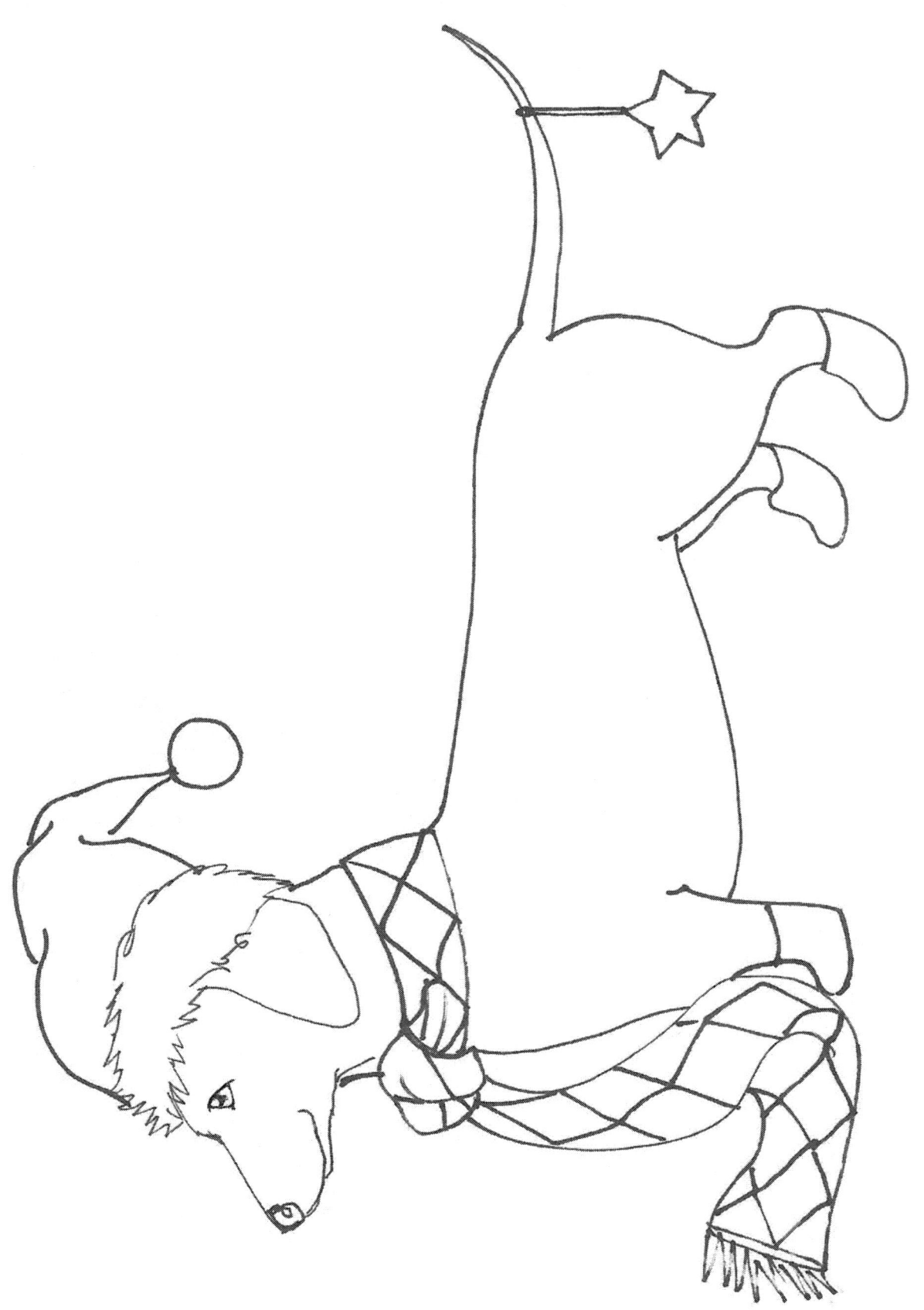

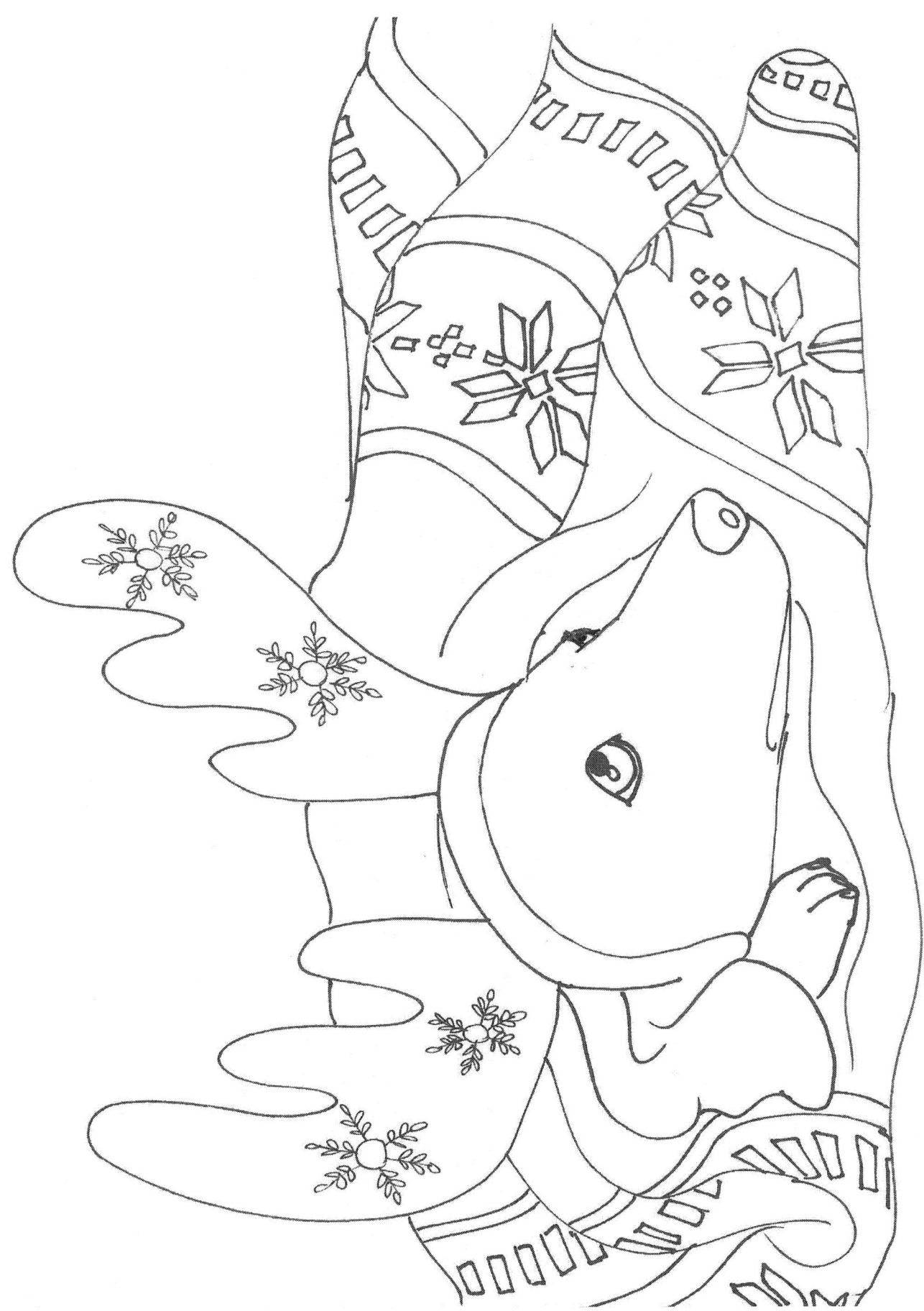

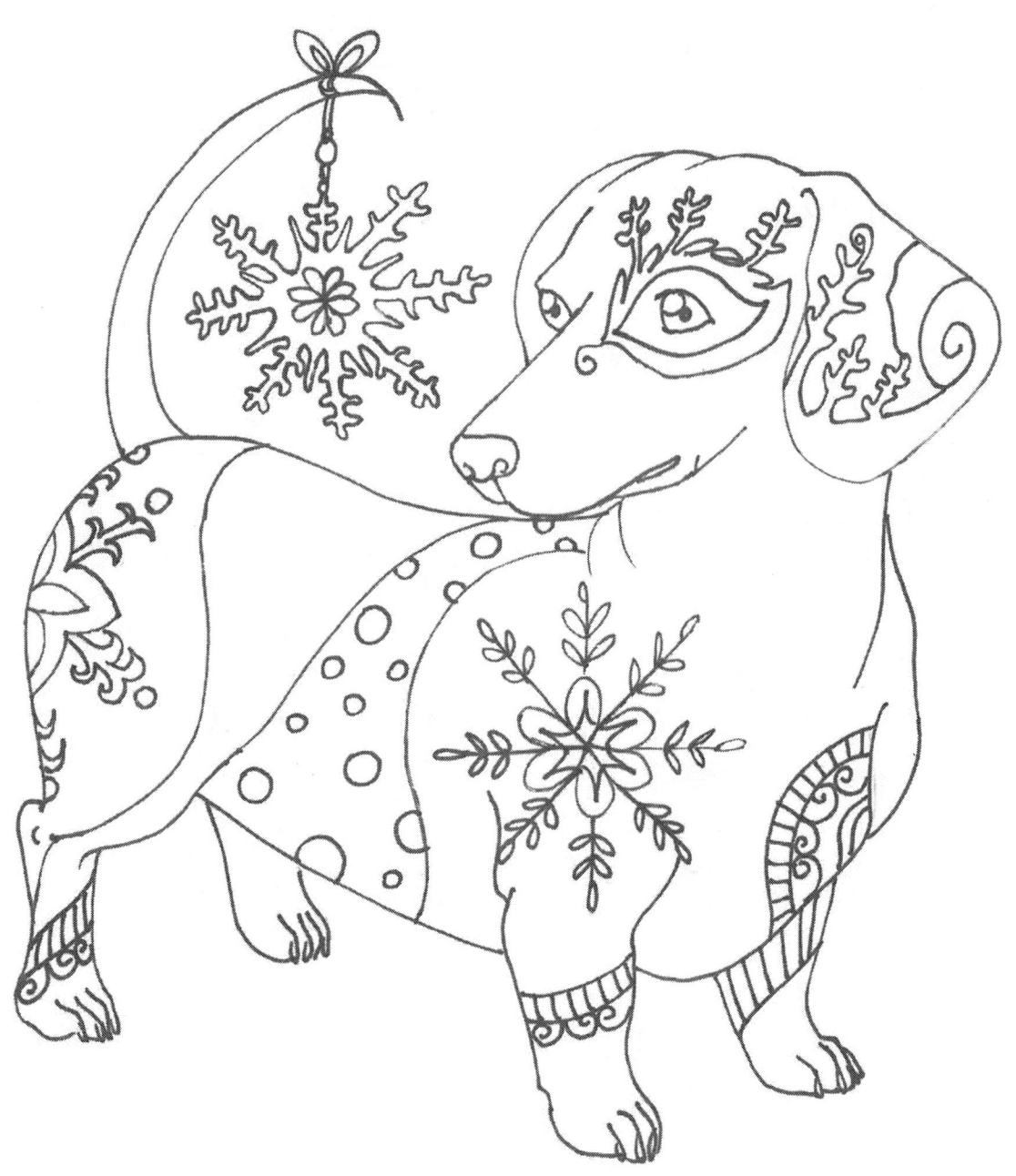

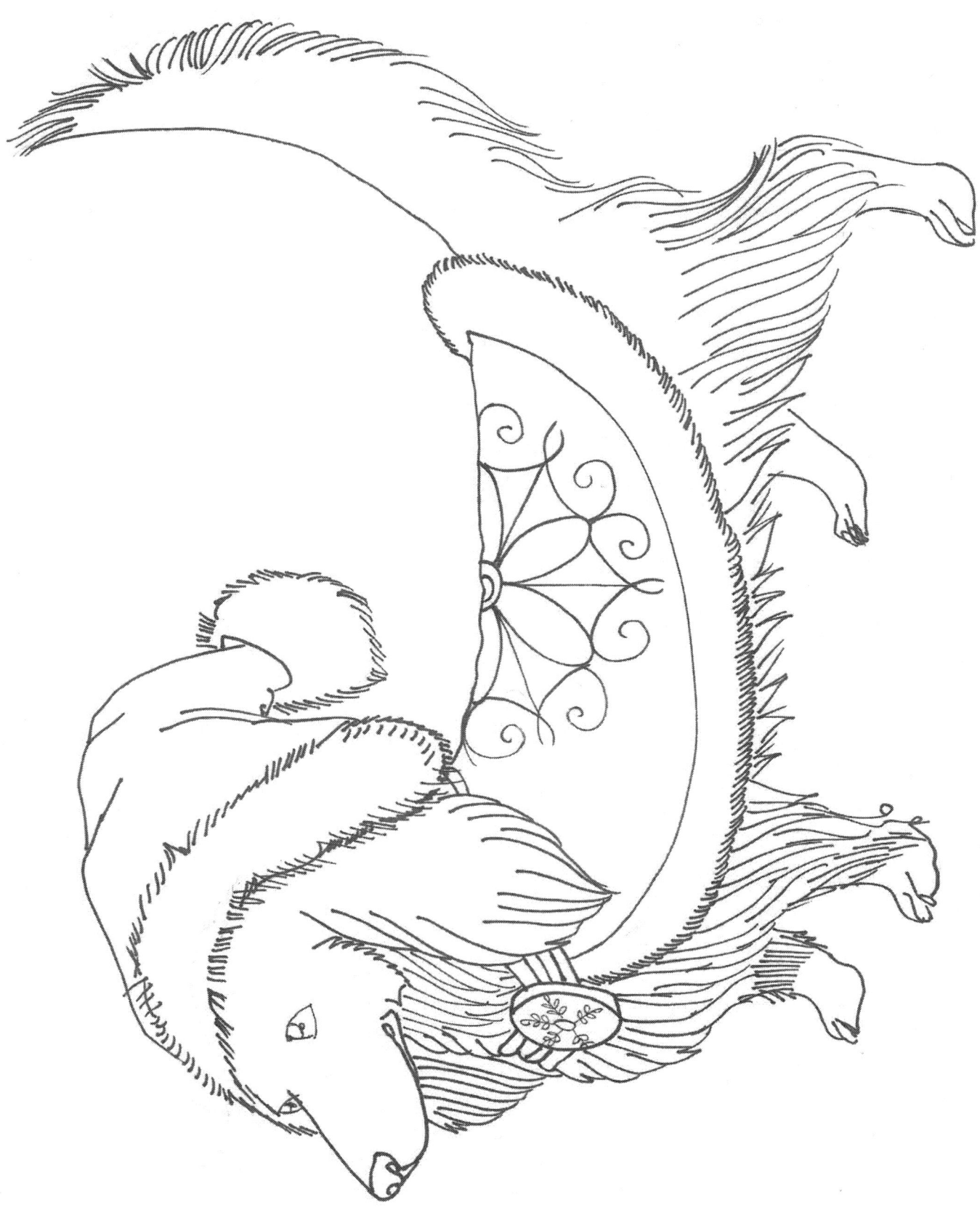

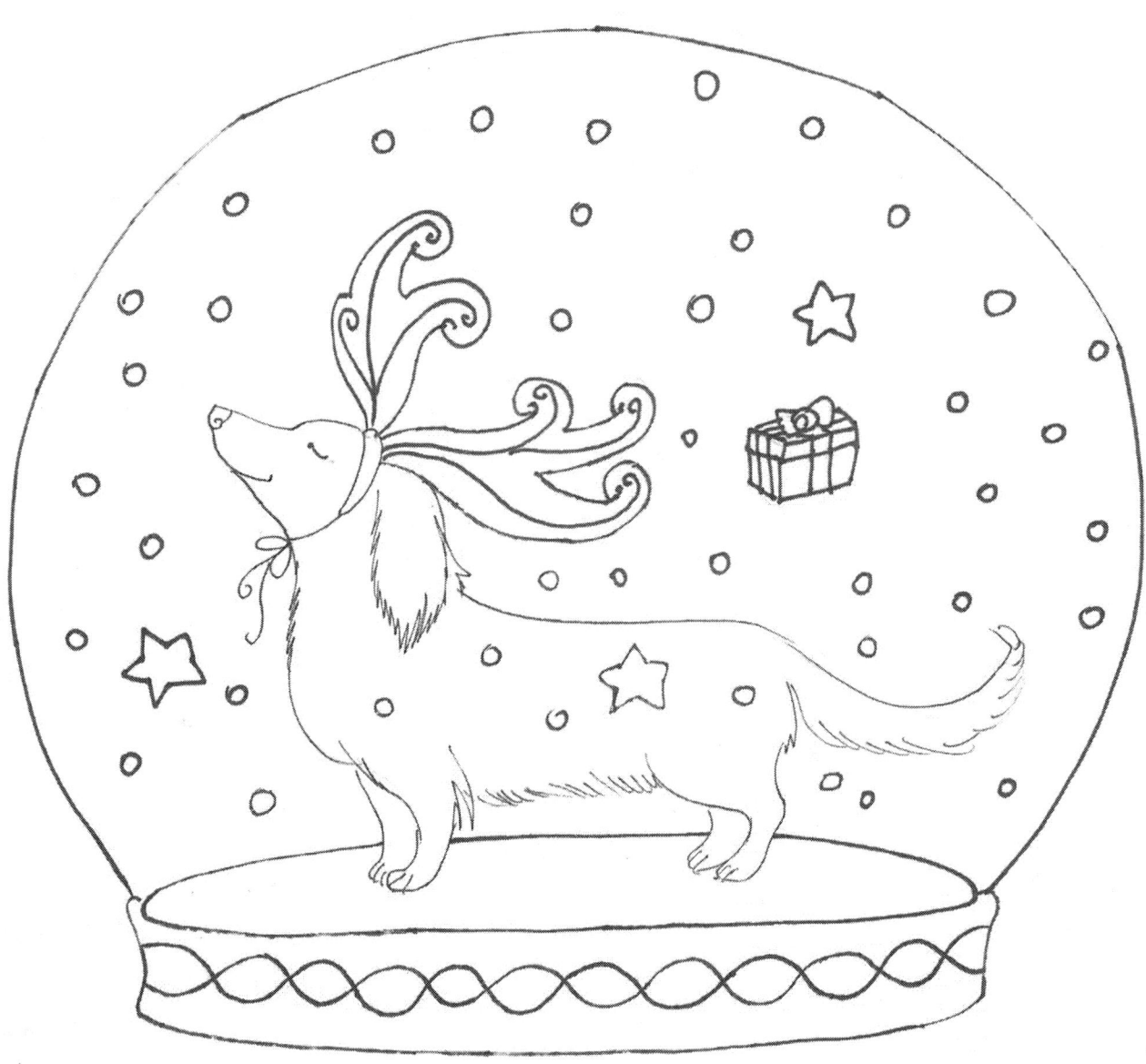

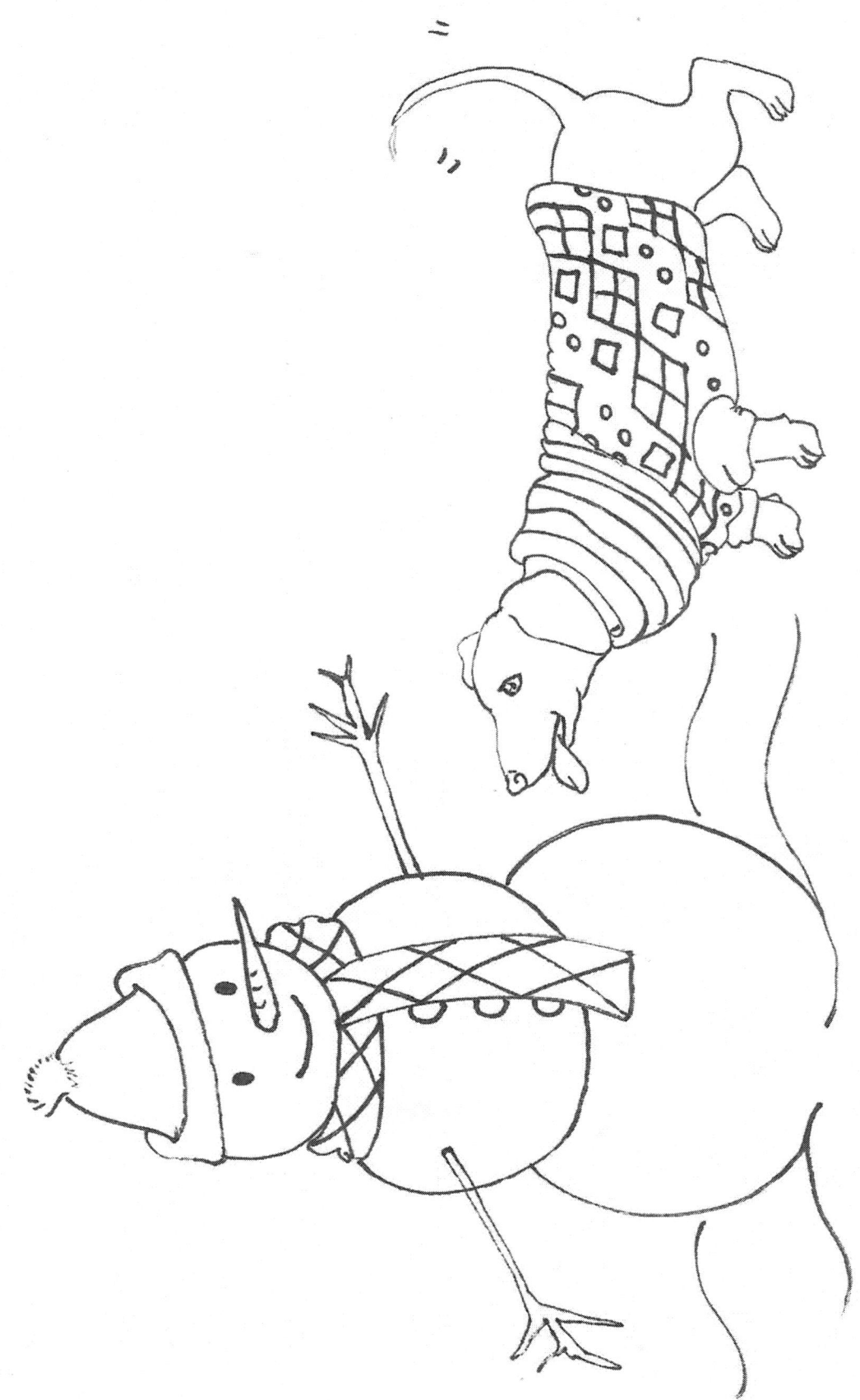

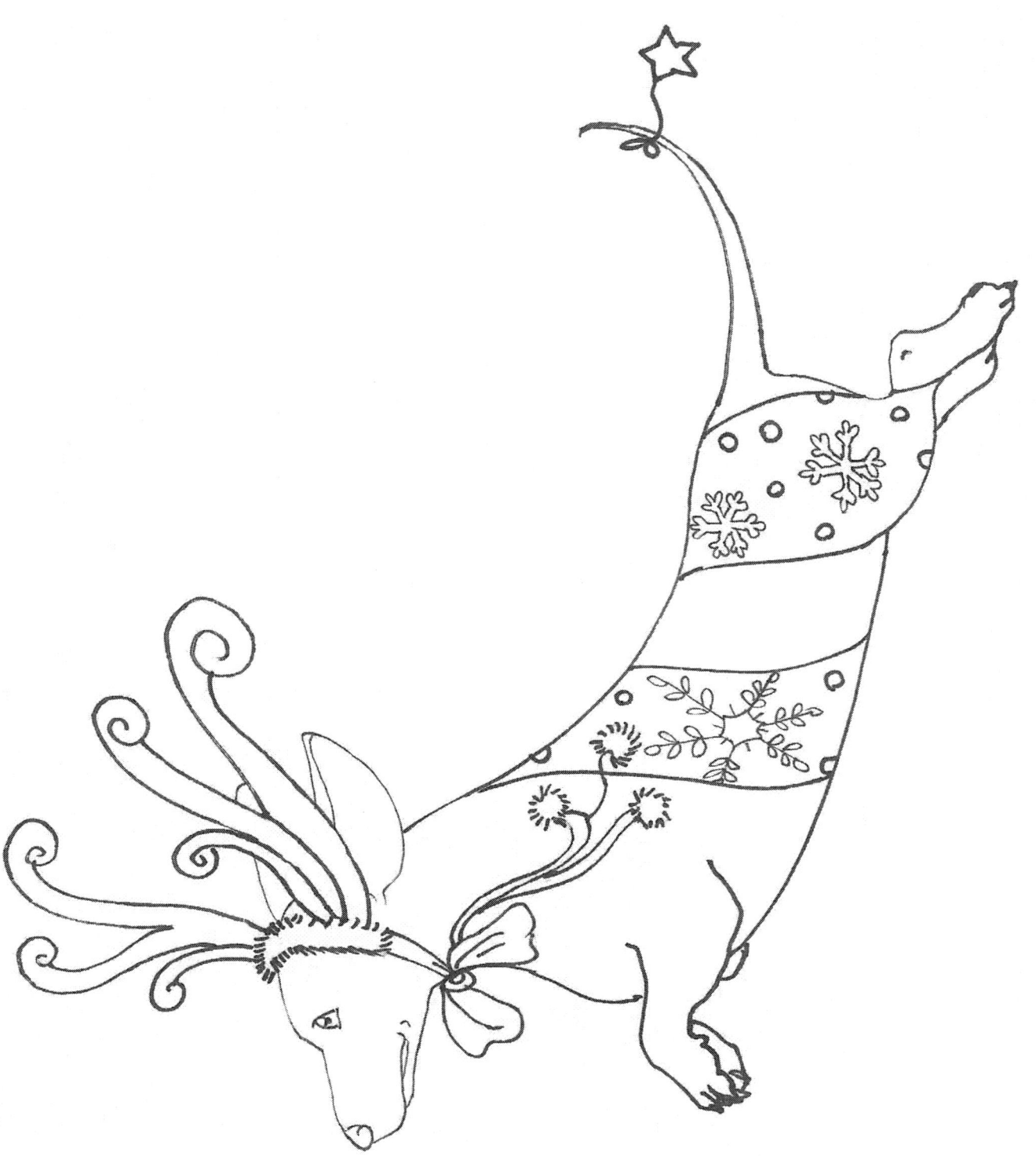

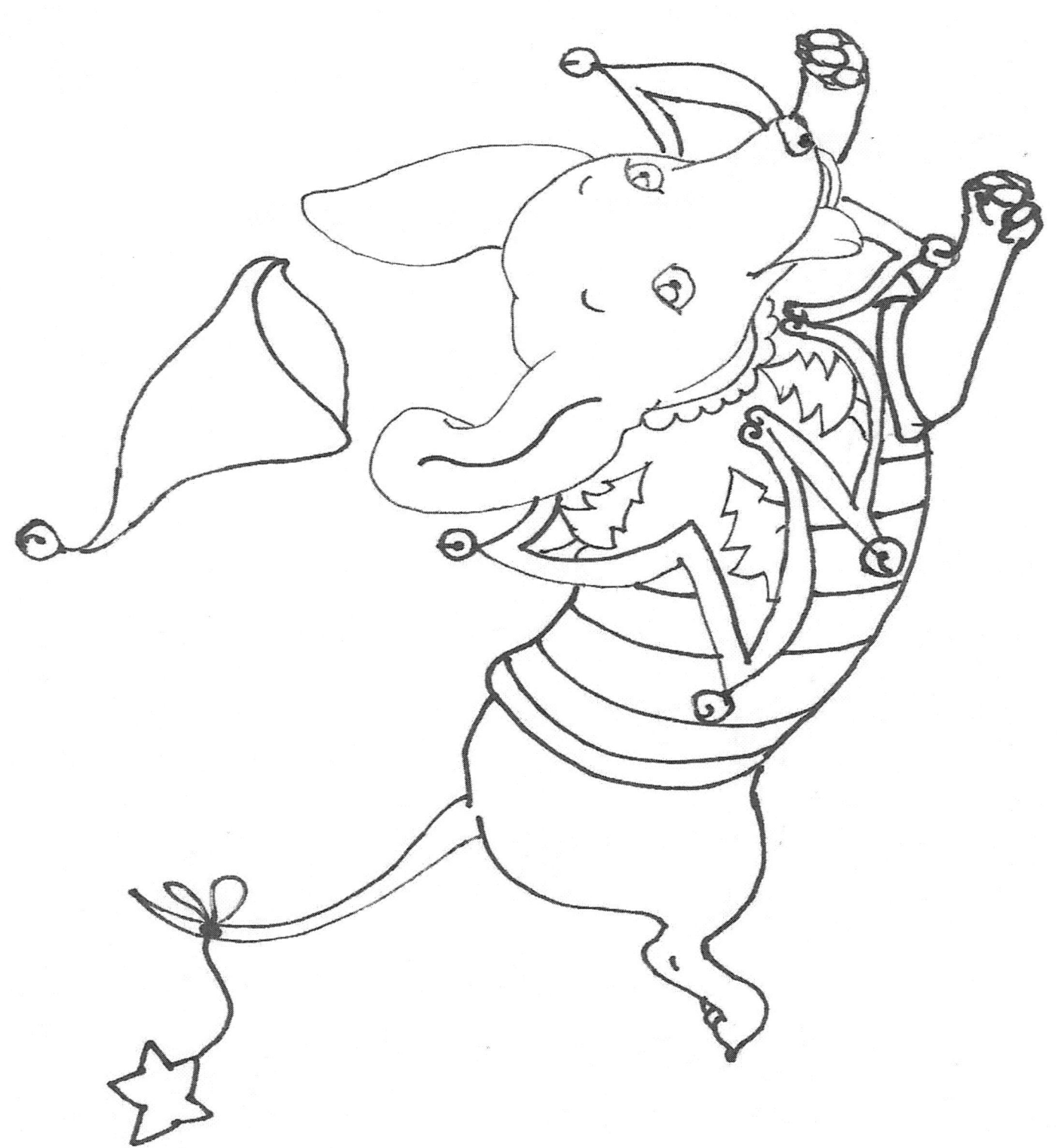

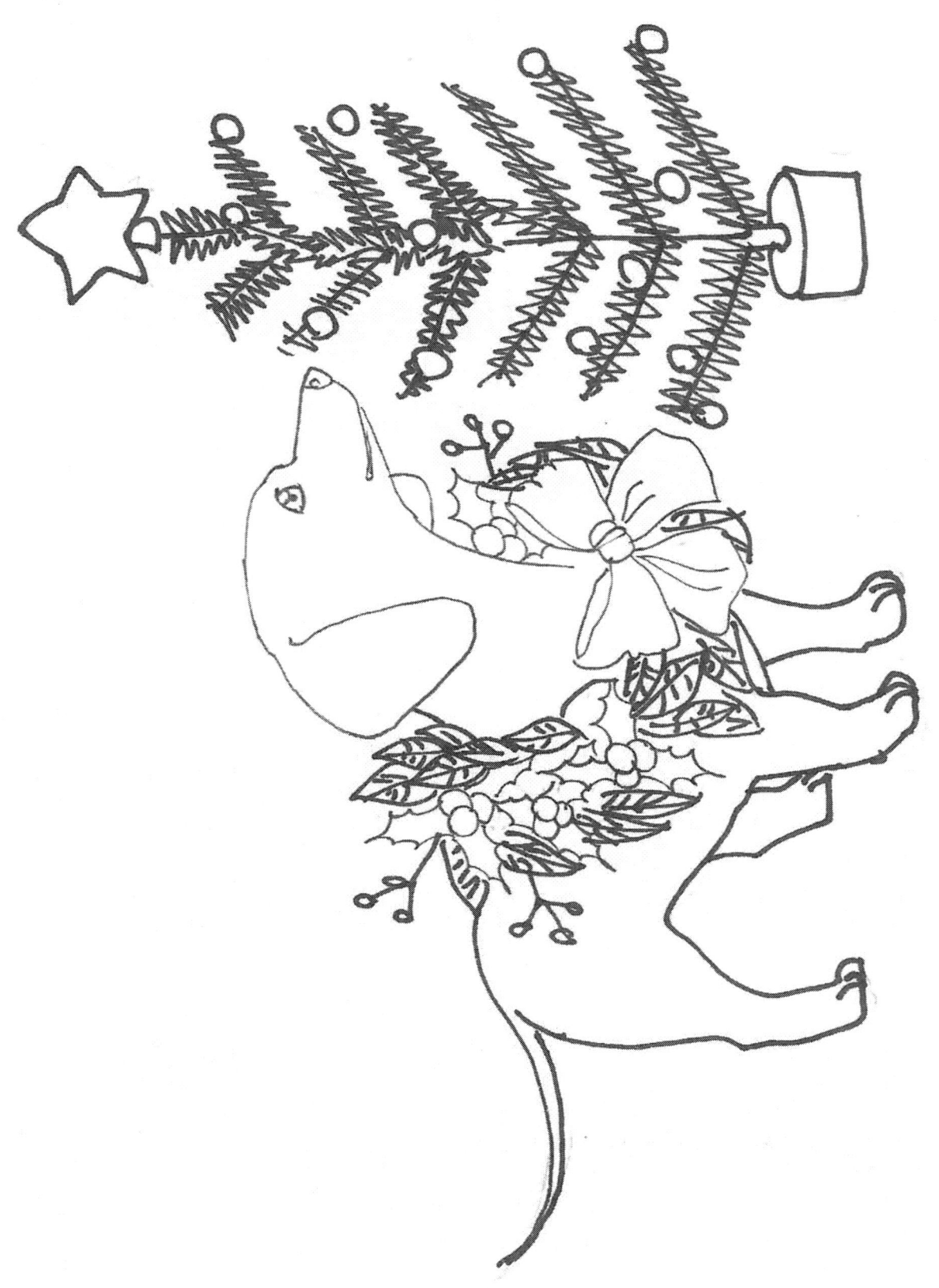

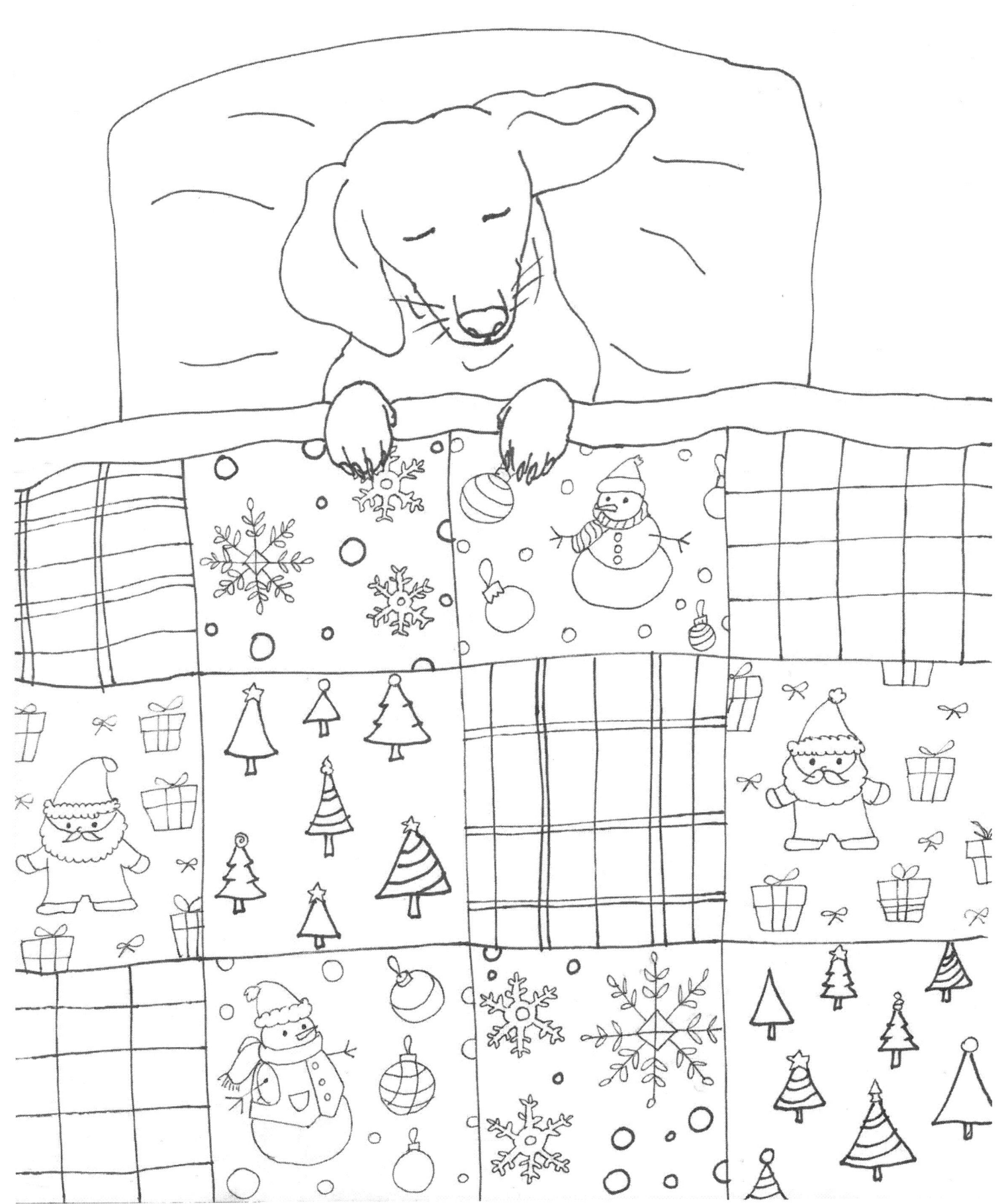

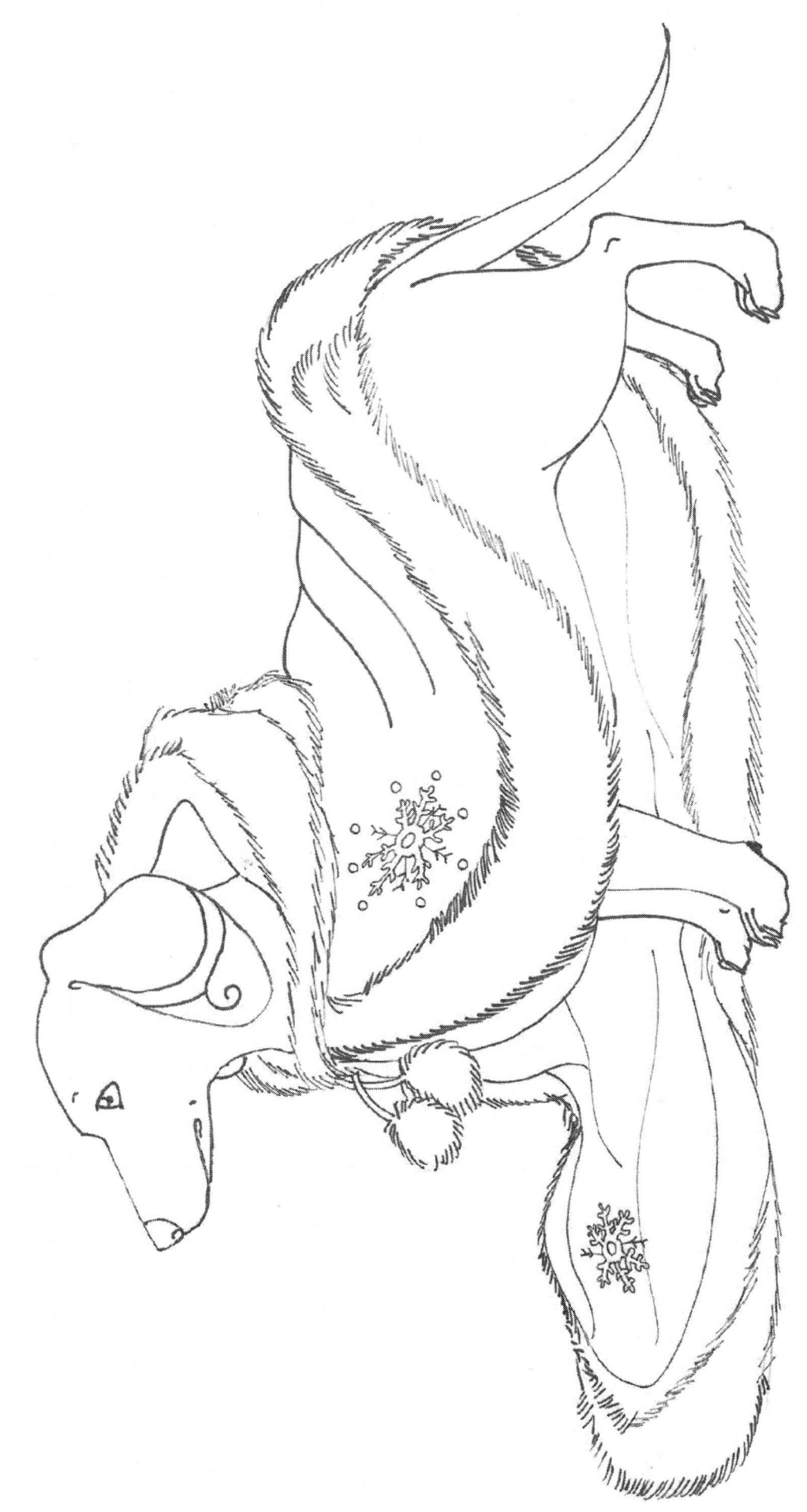

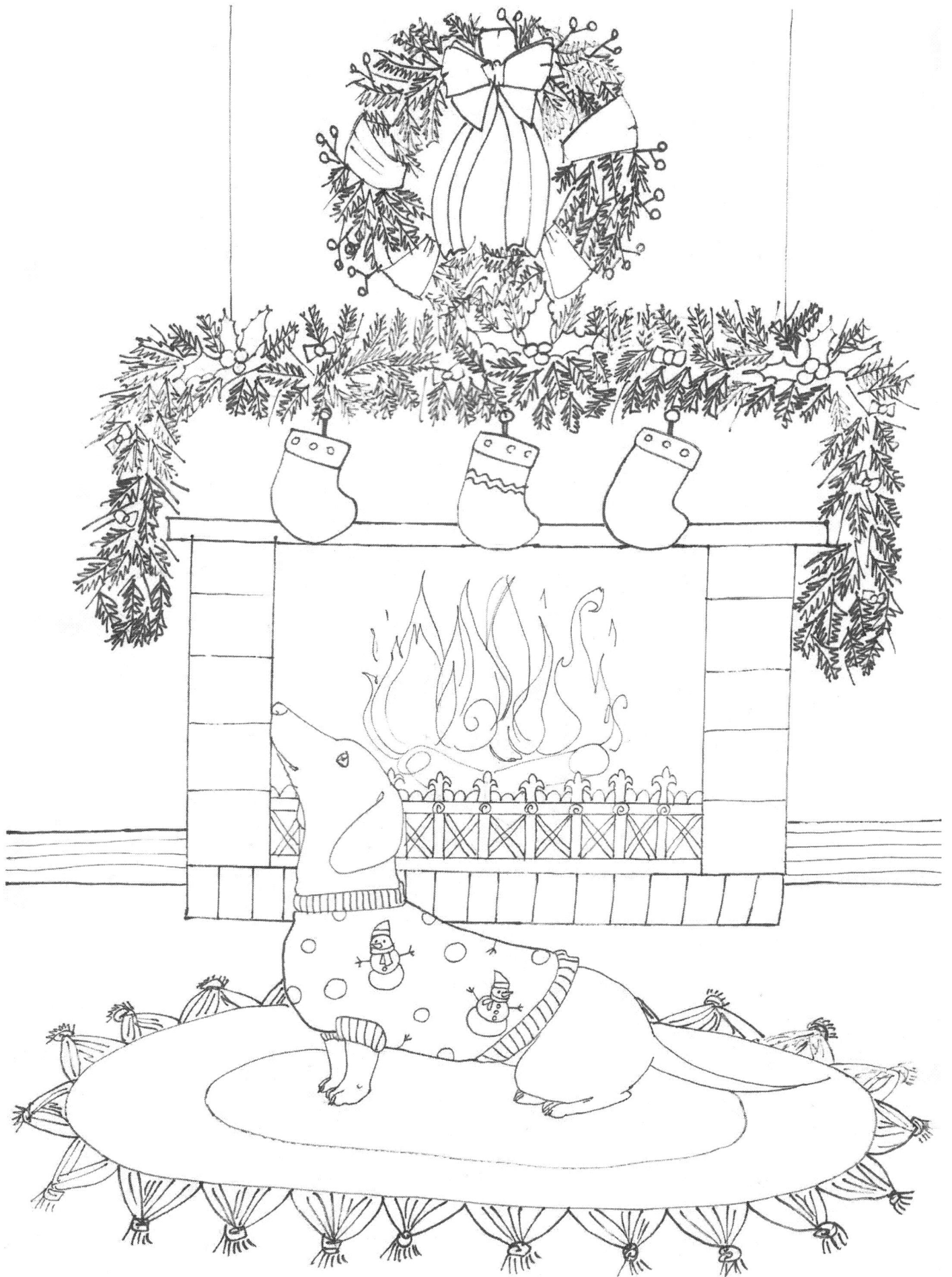

Printed in Poland
by Amazon Fulfillment
Poland Sp. z o.o., Wrocław